GOING WILD

W9-CTN-727

Amazing Animal Adventures
In Rivers

with Brian Keating

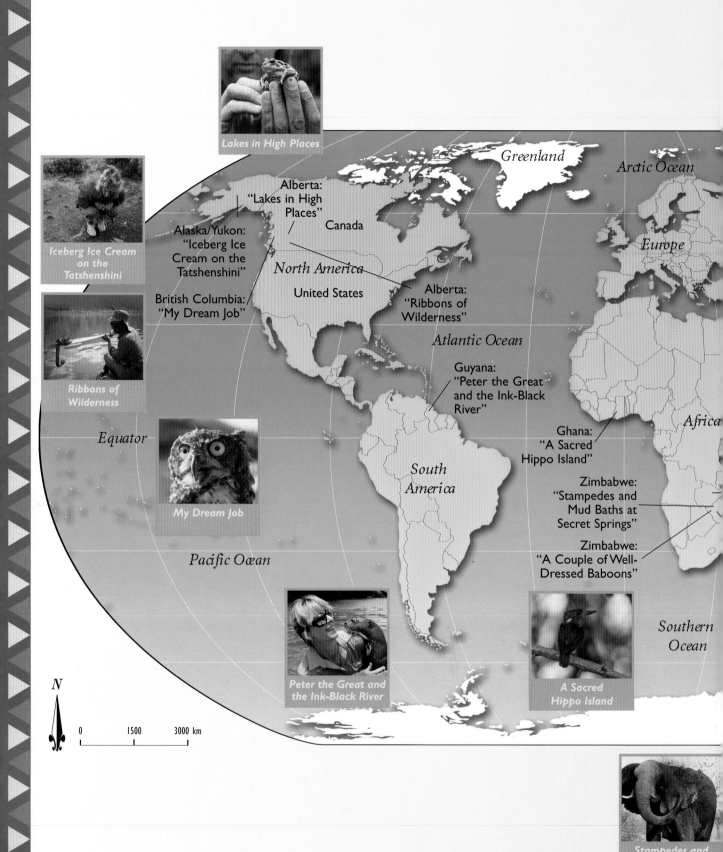

Lakes in High Places

Iceberg Ice Cream on the Tatshenshini

Ribbons of Wilderness

My Dream Job

Greenland

Arctic Ocean

Alberta: "Lakes in High Places"

Canada

Alaska/Yukon: "Iceberg Ice Cream on the Tatshenshini"

Europe

British Columbia: "My Dream Job"

North America

United States

Alberta: "Ribbons of Wilderness"

Atlantic Ocean

Africa

Equator

Guyana: "Peter the Great and the Ink-Black River"

Ghana: "A Sacred Hippo Island"

South America

Zimbabwe: "Stampedes and Mud Baths at Secret Springs"

Zimbabwe: "A Couple of Well-Dressed Baboons"

Pacific Ocean

Southern Ocean

N

0   1500   3000 km

Peter the Great and the Ink-Black River

A Sacred Hippo Island

Stampedes and Mud Baths at Secret Springs

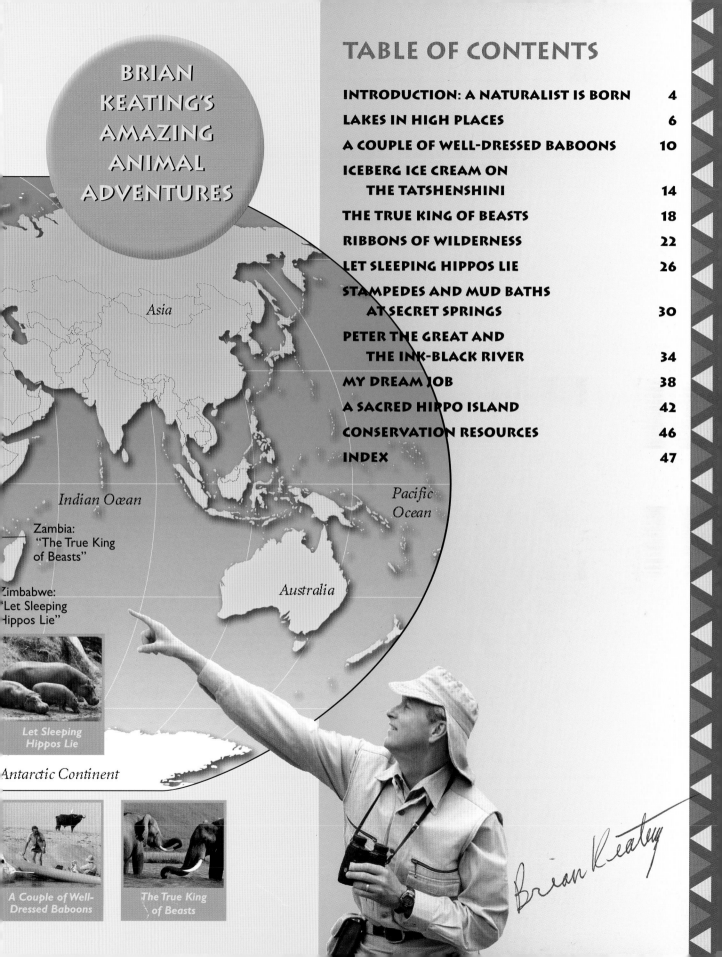

BRIAN KEATING'S AMAZING ANIMAL ADVENTURES

TABLE OF CONTENTS

Asia

Indian Ocean

Pacific Ocean

Zambia: "The True King of Beasts"

Zimbabwe: "Let Sleeping Hippos Lie"

Australia

Antarctic Continent

Let Sleeping Hippos Lie

A Couple of Well-Dressed Baboons

The True King of Beasts

Brian Keating

A NATURALIST IS BORN

Every little kid has an interest in running water, and I was no different. I can remember putting homemade boats in creeks and walking alongside them as they disappeared in the torrents and reappeared downstream. And in my early days of backpacking and camping, I remember gleefully camping beside creeks and rivers in the Bragg Creek, Alberta, area. I was endlessly fascinated by water rippling down and rolling over rocks.

Later, for a wedding gift, my brothers made my wife, Dee, and me a canoe. Every spring when the waters are high we canoe for a couple of weekends down prairie rivers. When it's the middle of winter in Alberta, everything is blanketed in snow, and the nights are long, I start to dream about that first canoe trip we always take in May.

Water fascinates me so much that Dee and I bought a house right beside the Bow River in Calgary, Alberta. We go down to the river, which is just beyond our backyard, and watch it just like we watch the screen at the movies. There's always something happening on the river, no matter what day of the week or time of the day.

When Dee and I are sitting by the river, a family of mergansers may come by or a little spotted sandpiper baby may struggle up onto our backyard, its mother nervously peeping in the water below. Just this morning I was inspecting a beaver trail in my backyard—he flattened out my marsh marigolds! Dee and I even bundle up in our backyard in winter and watch the river freeze solid in –30°C (–22°F). It's quite amazing how the water turns into a Slurpee before it freezes solid!

As part of my job as the Calgary Zoo's director of the Conservation Outreach Program, I have had the pleasure of visiting some of the greatest rivers and riparian areas (places near riverbanks) around the world. This has allowed me to have some unique experiences in water and to become better acquainted with the plants and animals existing around it. Some of these

Exploring the world's waters, above and below ground!

Your Own Backyard Adventure
Making a Bird Blind

In order to watch and photograph animals and birds up close, without disturbing them, I have often built wildlife watching "blinds." A blind can be anything from an elaborate, camouflaged hut in the forest to a simple, painted cardboard box near a birdfeeder or bird bath. The trick is to make your blind as invisible as possible—and it's easier than you think! Try making a simple bird blind by following the instructions below. You'll be amazed by the animals and birds you can watch on your school grounds or in your own backyard.

You will need:
- a cardboard box large enough for you to sit inside comfortably
- a pair of scissors
- green, brown, and black markers or paint; leaves, grasses, sticks, pinecones
- a pillow or small chair with a back

How to make the blind:
1. Draw a small window on one side of the box and cut the window out with your scissors.
2. Camouflage the outside of the box by using your brown, black, and green markers or paint. Draw trees and bushes. You can also glue leaves, sticks, and other organic elements to the box to really make it blend in.
3. Position your new bird blind near a full bird feeder or a bird bath with your window facing the feeder so you get a good, unobstructed view.
4. **ALWAYS** be sure to place the blind in an area free of cars or other potentially hazardous machinery. Never place it on a street, sidewalk, or driveway.

Viewing birds:
1. Go get a snack, something to drink, your binoculars, field guide, your journal, and that pillow or chair!
2. Crawl back into the bird blind and wait quietly for the birds to come. Be patient because it may take quite some time for the birds to get used to the box.
3. You can take a journal and some drawing pencils and sketch the birds you see to help you learn all of the markings that help make each bird different. Consider taking a camera into the blind—the best pictures of animals are those taken when they don't know you are there.

Hint: Set up a bird feeder or bird bath a least a week before you set up your blind. Then, set your blind up and leave it for a few days to allow the birds to get used to it.

adventures are contained in this book. I hope they do justice to my deep love and respect for rivers, and the lakes and ponds that are part of river systems. And I hope that my adventures inspire you to learn more about rivers and the wildlife living in and near them.

LAKES IN HIGH PLACES

One of the main reasons I enjoy living in Calgary, Alberta, is its closeness to the mountains. I moved to Calgary when I was 17 years old and, realizing how close those amazing mountains are, I quickly got into backpacking. My buddy, Derek, and I collected garbage bags full of pop cans from our high school (before recycling was something everyone did). We cashed in the pop cans, and in no time we had enough money to buy a tent, sleeping bags, and backpacks. Then we started exploring the mountain terrain around us.

Once you get over the idea that back-packing is hard work and you train your body to enjoy the work, the world is wide open. The more experience we gained back-packing weekend after weekend, the more we would diverge from the beaten path.

Derek and I used the trail systems to get through the forest and then up into the alpine. We found, and I still find, perfect alpine lakes, formed by glaciers in the middle of nowhere that often take a day or two to reach. There's not a huge diversity of creatures that live in the alpine, so it was always one of those catch-your-breath moments when we saw something flying, or walking, or hopping around.

This is the elk I photographed with Mount Assiniboine in the background. A bull elk's antlers will grow as long as 2 meters (6 ft.) and weigh as much as 14 kilograms (30 lb.).

One of the most surprising critters I have found in the alpine was a toad in a small, nameless alpine lake at the headwaters of Horsethief Creek, which eventually flows into the Columbia River. On the other side of the lake from where we were camping, glacier toes were calving ice cubes—it was that cold! But, here was this cold-blooded amphibian hopping around in the reeds and grasses along the edge of the lake. The water near the toad was so cold that there were still some slow-melting ice cubes from the glacier floating around it.

How the toad got up there is beyond me. Maybe the original tadpoles were caught in a grizzly bear's fur as the bear wandered from a lowland pond to the alpine lake. Or, maybe that toad was just an adventurous adult that hopped up to that area and was somehow managing to survive.

I started to understand a bit more about how the toad was making a living when I got down on my knees in the reeds to look at it. I could see that the air above the reeds and grasses was buzzing with all kinds of alpine flies. This toad could probably build enough body fat from

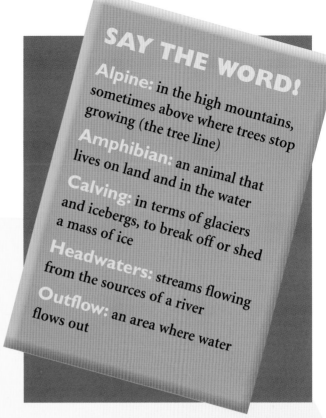

SAY THE WORD!

Alpine: in the high mountains, sometimes above where trees stop growing (the tree line)

Amphibian: an animal that lives on land and in the water

Calving: in terms of glaciers and icebergs, to break off or shed a mass of ice

Headwaters: streams flowing from the sources of a river

Outflow: an area where water flows out

them to do just fine, thank you very much, way up there in the cold.

Other creatures that sometimes patrol the water edges or the outflow creeks in the alpine are some specifically adapted birds, like dippers. Dippers, also called water oozles, are high-energy water birds. They prefer fast-moving creeks in which to find their dinner. So dippers will often claim the outflow area of a lake as part of their territory. These cool birds actually walk under water and pick off insects and

A toad, like this one, living near an alpine lake would have to survive a chilly, short summer and adapt to long winter hibernation in order to survive.

alpine. But there's not a lot of food in the alpine lakes for these fisher birds. Most alpine lakes don't have any fish in them, unless they've been introduced. The herons I've seen up there may have just been passing through. When they find no fish, they move on.

The areas around alpine lakes are gorgeous. Some remote alpine lakes have beautiful meadows around them. I hike into these quiet meadows from lakeside campsites to look for big wildlife like grizzly bears and elk. Elk often go to some of the hard-to-get-to areas to have their young.

I remember one time I was beside a babbling brook first thing in the morning photographing some flowers. The light was just starting to illuminate the landscape, and I looked up and there was this beautiful male elk with antlers in velvet. He was standing right in front of

In summer bighorn sheep can be found as high up in the alpine as 1,829–2,591 meters (6,000–8,500 ft.) in elevation. They don't require drinking water when vegetation is available and may only drink once in 3 days.

aquatic creatures that are living underneath the fissures and cracks of the lake ice. They bob up and down constantly and even more so when they are in whitewater outflows, or places where their calls could be drowned out by the sound of water gushing.

It seems that the way dippers communicate with each other is by bobbing—although to me it looks like they can't make a decision about whether or not to go into the water. Oh no, it's too cold, but gotta go in. Can't go in. Gotta go in. No, no, better step back. And so on! But really, the bobbing up and down is a sign to their youngsters and mates that they're okay, just keeping an eye on everyone.

Spotted sandpipers also like the outflow areas. I've even seen some herons in the

BRIAN'S NOTES

Some alpine lakes, called tarns, have no outflow at all, but they have something like a drain plug at their bottom that allows water to flow out below the ground. Sometimes you can find water coming out of the mountain when you're hiking. Often that water is from a tarn.

Dippers build globe-shaped nests that are usually wet on the outside, but the inside stays remarkably dry. Dippers usually use the same nest each year.

Like most water birds, dippers have many big preen glands throughout their feathers which help them stay waterproof in cold mountain streams. Unlike most water birds, though, dippers don't have webbed feet! They used their "toes" to grasp the bottom of river beds as they search for food.

Mount Assiniboine, one of the bigger mountains in Canada's Rockies. It was a stunning view! Those are the types of rewards one can have in these alpine locations.

Twice, my wife, Dee, and I have been lucky enough to have experiences with wolverines on high lakes, too. Wolverines are members of the mustelid family—so they are related to mink, weasels, and skunks—and they are rare creatures. Once we had skied up to a high alpine lake and were camping in the snow beside it. We noticed something dead on the lake. The ice on the surface was soft and mushy so we couldn't get out to look at what it was. But twice we saw a wolverine come in and feed on whatever was out there. It was exciting to see this secretive creature, even if it was from a distance.

These cold alpine lakes and streams really are the haunts of some fascinating creatures—animals and birds, and even some amphibians, that can survive in a chilly climate. I sometimes think that my first backpacking experiences to the alpine lakes in the Rockies set the course for me to become who I am today. It goes to show that it's never too early to start visiting the magnificent natural areas that may be right in your own backyard, just like I did.

A COUPLE OF WELL-DRESSED BABOONS

Dee and I have been traveling to Zimbabwe since 1982. Why? Because of a river. The Zambezi River in Zimbabwe and Zambia is one of the most exciting places I've ever spent time. It's a famous river because it creates Victoria Falls in Zimbabwe, one of the seven wonders of the natural world. I've canoed this wonderful river many times and I love it more every time I go.

Part of the Zambezi flows on the Zimbabwe side of the border between Zimbabwe and Zambia, through a place called a wilderness area. No roads are allowed in these areas (not even dirt tracks) so there are no vehicles.

When I get out of the canoe and walk out onto the banks and into the forest, I feel like I'm the only person on the planet. It's a place where you can climb a termite mound and do a 360-degree circle and count 7 or 8 species of large mammals: you may see some kudu or an eland over here, groups of impala or troops of baboons over there. There are probably some vervet monkeys sitting above you in the trees. Back in the water, the sound of grunting hippos is a constant companion, and stealthy crocodiles the size of your canoe sometimes make appearances, too.

The forest that meets the Zambezi is also a place where elephants roam. In this ancient riparian forest there are acacia trees, called winter thorn trees because they leaf out in the dry season and lose their leaves in the rainy season. These trees are also called apple-ring acacia because they produce neat-looking, spiral-shaped pods. These pods can often be found on the forest floor. Elephants eat these pods like potato chips. They pick them up with the tips of their trunks and flick the

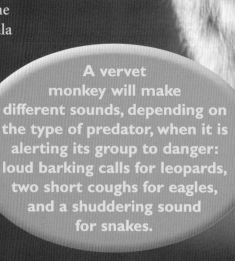

A vervet monkey will make different sounds, depending on the type of predator, when it is alerting its group to danger: loud barking calls for leopards, two short coughs for eagles, and a shuddering sound for snakes.

We watched this elephant along the banks of the Zambezi for hours. He would rear up on his back legs and pull branches down with his trunk so he could eat the leaves. After he moved off, antelope would come in and browse on the vegetation left by the elephant.

BRIAN'S NOTES

Zimbabwe is known for some of the best lightning storms in the world. It is in the Guinness Book of World Records for the most number of people killed by one lightning strike.

When impala want to show off their health and exuberance to potential predators, they pronk. They bounce up and down like they're on pogo sticks. Essentially, they're saying, "Go ahead lion, try to take me down, you're going to have a heck of a time because i'm so full of good energy and i'm so healthy that i'll really give you a run for your money!"

crunchy treats into their mouths. The pods provide much-needed protein and nutrients when the season is dry and there is little food.

An elephant will go from tree to tree eating the pods that have spilled on the ground. If there aren't enough on the ground, the elephant will shake the whole tree back and forth with its forehead. The tree sounds like a gigantic rattle being shaken, and soon pods cascade to the ground. These fallen pods not only feed the elephants that shake them loose, but also other creatures that wait until the elephants have left to pick up the remaining pods.

When exploring the Zambezi and the forests around it, Dee and I start each day by taking a moment to watch and listen to Africa wake up. Then we enter the water in canoes. First thing in the morning, we don't feel the need to paddle. We just sit there in the bucket seats of the canoe and watch the scenery go by as the current carries us down the river.

The closer we get to the Mana Pools National Park, the more wildlife we see.

When antelope, such as these impala, are in danger they let out a bark. It's a really strong, powerful bark that makes you perk up your ears and raises the hairs on the back of your neck. Because you know something scared them. Lion?

We usually surprise a lot of elephants while paddling the Zambezi River. Some put their heads up and their ears out to let us know that this is their land. We quietly drift by, like well-dressed, submissive baboons floating on a log.

Once, we paddled around a corner to find two elephant bulls horsing around in the water. It looked like they were having a mud fight! We grabbed on to a hanging branch to hold the canoe in one place. Then we watched for half an hour as the elephants splashed in the water, oblivious to our presence.

Judging by the dung and the number of animal tracks on the sand bank closest to those 2 elephants, we figured it was probably an epicenter for wildlife. We decided to set up our tent there. Sure enough, we had elephants coming and going all night. The way we set up our tent on top of the steep riverbank, we could see the elephants' huge foreheads when they walked past us.

We saw buffalo standing near the river looking at us looking at them. And when a buffalo looks at you, you feel pretty small! They walk with such confidence, attitude, and dignity.

With so much life around, there are always lots of lions, too. There's something very exciting about paddling down a narrow channel and looking up into the eyes of a lion.

One year on the last night of our canoe trip, we finished off the trip at one of my favorite camps, a place called Chikwenya. It was dark when we decided to borrow a vehicle from the owner of the camp and go for a drive.

We came across 6 lions as skinny as greyhounds. I was holding a floodlight, and at that moment I shone it ahead to find about 100 snorting impala standing there with their eyes beaming like green marbles. In amongst the impala was one kudu. We turned off the floodlight. We didn't want to give the lions an unfair advantage. Then, we sat there in the darkness and listened.

The air exploded with sound. The antelope were barking like crazy, baboons were screaming up in the trees because they knew lions were near, and all of a sudden we heard the antelope running. Then we heard the unbelievable sound of the lions taking down the kudu. At that point I turned on the light, and we saw the final moments of the kill.

We drove up near it, and for the next while we watched these lions consume the kudu. Within half an hour, the kudu was just some skin, bones, and connective tissue. Coming across this scene was just one of those incredible lucky moments and a dramatic way to end our trip.

The Zambezi River is an amazing part of the world, and it's still wild. When canoeing, you're always on the river by yourself even though there may be a group of canoeists a day behind you and a group a day ahead of you. I think canoeing this river is one the best wildlife experiences in all of Africa. It's a powerful place to experience, and it's one of those places that makes you feel small and humble and privileged to be alive.

ICEBERG ICE CREAM ON THE TATSHENSHINI

A few years ago I was asked to be the naturalist on a rafting trip on the Tatshenshini River, which flows through Yukon Territory in Canada, into Alaska, USA, and out to the Pacific Ocean. This very dynamic and dramatic river is famous because it is so beautiful and wild. It flows right through the St. Elias Mountain Range, which has some of North America's highest mountains. There are no roads and only a couple of hunters' cabins along the way out to the ocean.

On this rafting trip, we got into a big rubber raft in the highlands around Whitehorse, Yukon, and 10 days later we got spit out at the other end in the ocean near Dry Bay, Alaska. In between Whitehorse and the Pacific, the river races along. When we stopped to camp and hike

along the river, we were constantly amazed and thankful for how pristine the landscape was.

The area around the Tatshenshini River seems untouched by people partly because of the people who hike and canoe there. The company I went with was called Canadian Rivers Expeditions. It's one of the first tour companies in North America to implement the policy that whatever you pack in you pack out. This even includes your own body waste! This practice is called no-trace camping.

When you think about it, there are usually about 18 people in each rafting group going

The ice we took from the Alsek Lake berg to make ice cream.

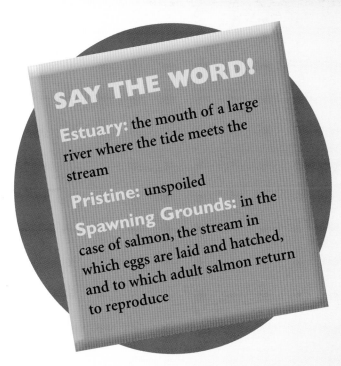
on 3 little legs. When it came time to put out the campfire, 2 guys would put on welders' gloves, lift up this red-hot cauldron, walk over to the river, and gently lower it into the river and douse all the coals. We weren't scorching the ground, and we weren't leaving behind any burnt wood.

No-trace camping is important because it helps to instill a respect for the land and wildlife living on the land. Every time we got out of the raft it became a bit of a contest to see who could find the first grizzly bear footprint. We found grizzly tracks in the mud beside the river every time we stopped, even if it was just for a quick break. We seldom saw the bears themselves and, when we did, only from a distance. But in one clear creek we did get to see a grizzly bear's delight: salmon swimming upstream!

down the Tatshenshini. And there are many groups, each going down the same river and using the same campsites night after night. That's bound to produce a lot of waste! So, we brought along a couple of military containers used for storing ammunition that had tough rubber seals around their openings. Whenever we stopped to set up camp, the first thing we did was open up this ammo box. We'd put a toilet seat on it and then set up a shelter around it. We could then sit and look out over the landscape on our "throne" as we made our deposit. Before we left a camp, we would put the lid back on our toilet and clamp down the seals before putting it back in the raft.

Setting an example like this for other tour companies rafting the same river was very important to Canadian Rivers Expeditions. Even our campfires were built on steel dishes raised

As a glacier grinds its way over rocks, it pulverizes the rock underneath into a flourlike substance called "rock flour." Because of the density of rock flour in the Tatshenshini River, the water is virtually white.

Salmon have always fascinated me because they live all their adult lives in the ocean. Then they swim up the same stream where they were born to lay their eggs. After they lay and fertilize the eggs, both the males and females die. Bears and eagles then eat their carcasses. This was the first time I had ever seen salmon swimming upstream, and it was very exciting to watch.

Usually what we saw of grizzly bears was what they left behind: their tracks!

While on this rafting trip we were also able to do some great hiking when we settled in for 2-night camps. We walked high into the alpine and saw goats and pikas. We also climbed up onto a glacier where we explored how it worked and how it had changed the landscape. Then, we had a 2-night stay at a place called Alsek Lake.

This lake is surrounded by huge glaciers that are all calving icebergs into the water. We camped there hoping to see some large chunks of ice fall off the glacier toe. We weren't disappointed. We watched a huge glacier iceberg roll over in the water. In the process it set up a wave that washed onto shore a few minutes afterward and pushed ice chunks a long way up the beach. As this iceberg rolled over, we saw it change from deep blue (because all the air pockets and fractures in this glacier ice were filled with water) to almost milky white in just a few minutes as the water drained out of it.

Then, we got into our rafts and rowed to the middle of the lake, looking for some clean ice to bring back to camp. We had brought an ice cream maker along with us, so the ice we found on the lake, which was perhaps 10,000 years old, was an ingredient in the ice cream we enjoyed later that night.

The next day, our group left the lake for our last float down to the ocean. It was an exciting moment when we came into the estuary and we could see the open ocean. We knew the next stop would be Japan or Northern Russia if we didn't go ashore. Finally our chartered airplane landed on a dirt strip. We collapsed the rafts that we used, took our canisters full of human waste, and loaded everything onto the plane.

At the end of this incredible trip, we flew

A face of ice about 13 kilometers (8 mi.) wide encircles Alsek Lake, which is filled with huge icebergs. It was amazing to paddle through them.

over parts of the Tatshenshini River to see it from the air. We flew right over the glacier that we had watched calve into Alsek Lake earlier that day. The water was awash with icebergs. It's always exciting to view things from another perspective! But from any perspective, whether from a raft, on foot, or in the air, the Tatshenshini River trip is one that I'll never forget!

BRIAN'S NOTES

salmon have the smell of their birth stream imprinted in their brains. This guides them "home." It can be a very long journey. Some salmon have to swim thousands of miles or jump over waterfalls to fight their way against the current. When they reach their destination, they have barely enough energy to lay or fertilize eggs before they die. Only the fittest salmon survive to reach their spawning grounds.

THE TRUE KING OF BEASTS

Nature exploration is very dramatic and exciting but it can rip your heart out, too. You cannot always be in a wonderful, pristine wild area—sometimes you experience the downside of human contact with wildlife, too. At the same time, there are usually magical moments that help to balance the low ones—and this is exactly what happened one summer when Dee and I were paddling in Africa.

We were canoeing in Zambia on the Zambezi River. In those days, Zambia was rife with poaching. We often heard rifle shots as we paddled along. One day we noticed vultures tracking above us. They were dropping straight down out of the sky. It looked like they were parachuting down. We knew that something big was dead.

We beached the canoe and cautiously walked into the woods. As we walked, we were always on guard for lions on a kill. All of a sudden a hyena ran this way and another hyena ran that way. We looked with our binoculars through the tangled bush, and we could see a dead elephant.

We watched the carcass for a long time. Slowly, so we wouldn't offend any lions that might be there, we worked our way in and went right over to it. It was one of the most heartbreaking scenes I have ever seen. The elephant's face had been chopped off, and the tusks were gone. Poachers had killed it.

We could tell the carcass was several days old. The lions had opened it up and animals had been feeding on it for quite a long time. A lot of the meat was gone, but it was very clear that the face had been hacked off with an axe. There's nothing more dead than a dead elephant. Elephants

An elephant's trunk has more than 40,000 muscles—more muscles than you have in your whole body!

are so big and majestic, so powerful and confident. They are the true king of beasts.

To see a dead elephant is a shocking thing, especially when it has been killed for greed. We found another carcass just down from there on the river that had probably been dead for 2 months. I could see AK47 bullet holes in the skull and in many of the long bones. It takes about 50 or 60 of these shots to pummel an elephant for it to even drop to its knees.

That was a very low period for us. Fortunately, most of the poaching has been eliminated in Africa thanks to the Ivory Ban established in 1989. African countries taking part in the ban made scenes of death like the one I just described available to people all over the world. This encouraged people not to buy ivory or other animal products that resulted from poaching.

On the opposite side of the emotional scale, we had one of our most wonderful moments on the Zambezi River on the very same day that we saw the dead elephants. Late in the afternoon we came across

BRIAN'S NOTES

Elephants will sometimes twine their trunks around those of other elephants. They also put the tips of their trunks into each other's mouths. This action demonstrates tremendous trust and friendship, and it probably gives each elephant an idea of what the other has been eating lately! This is called an "elephant handshake."

When you see a vulture circling above you, that doesn't mean there is a kill down below. That means they're looking for a kill or something to eat.

SAY THE WORD!

Desolate: deserted and barren

Poaching: illegal hunting, especially if the animal being hunted is protected by law

Rife: abundant, widespread

a big bull elephant, probably 60 years old, feeding on water plants along the edge of the river. We watched him for a while, then 4 other big bull elephants came out of the bushes and joined him. I'm sure they had communicated and planned to meet up for a drink and a browse on the vegetation. They were like an old boys club!

They were playing and drinking together, and then the big bull climbed into the water. He strode in right up to his forehead, then the water rolled over him. It was so hot we could almost hear the elephant's skin sizzle when he climbed in. Then he came up with his tusks gleaming white, and we could see the excitement in his eyes. He looked so happy and the air was filled with anticipation. The other 4 bulls lined up on the river's edge. It was as if they had taken a ticket from a government passport office and were waiting for their number to be called.

The big bull reached up to one of the bulls. He wrapped his trunk around his friend's trunk and pulled him into the water. Then the big bull grabbed the next one and the next and then finally the last elephant, pulling them into the refreshing water. We had dozens of tons of cavorting elephants all black with Zambezi water running off them. And the crack of their wet tusks clacking together sounded like wet billiard balls.

An elephant's trunk weighs about 182 kilograms (400 lb.) and is so precise that it can pick up a single grain of rice. It can also be used as a snorkel when swimming!

Elephants will visit the dead bodies of fellow elephants. A big bull I once watched stood near a fallen friend, sniffing every square centimeter of it with the tip of his trunk. When a younger elephant came over to see what he was doing, the big bull turned and pushed the youngster away. Maybe the bull was remembering the fallen elephant and wanted to spend some quiet time.

Poaching and the Ivory Ban

During the worst poaching years in Africa, from 1980 to 1989, 100,000 elephants a year were disappearing from the continent. Scientists thought that elephants would be extinct by the turn of the century. But then a world-wide Ivory Ban went into effect in 1989. People around the world were moved by profoundly disturbing and disgusting images of dead elephants with hacked-off faces. People realized that if they bought ivory, they killed elephants. The blood was on everyone's hands. The ivory ban was a very powerful and very effective tool in protecting Africa's elephant populations. It's rare now to find an elephant killed for its ivory, but it still happens occasionally.

Although the Ivory Ban helped to stop poaching in much of Africa, poaching elephants for ivory continues today in countries like Zimbabwe. African elephants are listed as a threatened species by some sources and an endangered species by others.

Male elephants leave their families when they are about 13 years old. When they leave the social group, they form loose associations with other male elephants where they learn to become adult males.

After more than 2 hours, some unheard communication between them signaled the end of the fun. The big bull turned and started to walk over to Zambia and the other bulls followed, one after the other.

Dee and I hadn't spoken a word to each other during that time. We were full of adrenaline, sitting with these animals so close that the wake they created actually rocked our canoe. We were just exhausted from the experience. When the elephants left, we pushed off and let the current carry us to the next island where we set up camp.

It was one of the best days we've had, enjoying the privilege of watching such exciting elephant interaction. It was also one of the worst days, finding the dead elephants. What a contrast of emotions it was for us!

RIBBONS OF WILDERNESS

Canoeing is one of my favorite ways to explore river systems and the land around them. I love it because if I'm on the river without a headwind, the river is just like a magic carpet moving me through incredible landscapes.

The landscapes around rivers are almost always amazing. You see, rivers are dynamic beasts that flood in the spring and react to torrential rainstorms or rapid melts in the mountains. Riverbanks are not the best places for people to build. If you build a house beside a river, eventually it will get washed away because rivers flood. That's the bottom line. So rivers are often ribbons of wilderness.

Over the last 25 years, Dee and I have canoed virtually every stretch of canoeable river from Red Deer, Alberta, south to the US border and east to the Saskatchewan border. On maps, we look for areas where there are coulees and good river or creek systems that meet a main river. I also sometimes rent a small plane and fly out above the southern Alberta rivers to find new places to explore. By paddling I can get into places where there are no houses, no roads or a dirt track at best, and only the odd cow. There are wonderful landscapes to explore, and a canoe will help you get there.

We spent 8 days canoeing the South Saskatchewan River a few years ago. That is about twice as much time as you need to do the stretch of river we wanted to cover. But we

We found this tired and cold rattlesnake attempting to swim across the river. I carefully scooped him up on my paddle and took him to shore. Because he was so cold, he was easy to transport and photograph.

Burrowing owls have long, thin legs like little stilts that help them peer up from their burrows across the prairie.

wanted to explore all of the grand coulees that enter into the main river system. The coulees are unstable sloped areas with glacial till or silt that shifts so you can't really build roads on them, unless you are prepared to build a new road every year! Farmers certainly don't like to build houses in these areas, so when we're hiking in coulees, it's like we're hiking in the prairies the way they were a thousand years ago. The neat thing about coulees is there are always blind corners and pathways and trails made by mule deer or cattle. The chances of happening upon wildlife are very good.

On this trip, we encountered several rattlesnakes including the biggest rattlesnake I have ever found. Dee and my buddies were at the camp getting organized, but I had this need to go for a walk and find out what was beyond where the riverine forest ended. I walked away from the river, into the prairie, and I found this rattlesnake that was as thick around as my wrist. I don't usually handle poisonous snakes. I would rather photograph them quietly

than cause them stress, but I wanted my friends to see it.

Everyone was back at the camp, and I knew that if I left, the snake wouldn't be there when I returned with my friends. I carefully captured the snake and walked it back to camp to show everyone. When I walked into camp with this meter-long rattlesnake, you

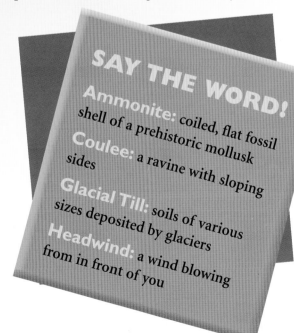

SAY THE WORD!

Ammonite: coiled, flat fossil shell of a prehistoric mollusk

Coulee: a ravine with sloping sides

Glacial Till: soils of various sizes deposited by glaciers

Headwind: a wind blowing from in front of you

23

Dawn Chorus in the Month of May

You can spot the most amazing birds in Alberta's riparian forests—most of them are birds that come north from the tropics to feast on our summer bugs! Catbirds, brown thrashers, yellow warblers, meadowlarks, lark buntings, red-winged blackbirds, yellow-rumped and Wilson's warblers, black and white warblers, American redstarts, and Baltimore orioles are some of the many birds that can be seen in May near the rivers of southern Alberta.

Dee and I plan our first 3-day canoe trip for May when the runoff is at its best. We like to be on a river somewhere in southern Alberta around the third week in May to watch the pulse of migrating birds fly through. At the crack of dawn we'll sit and listen to the first birds start to call, enjoying the beautiful symphony filling the air. It's called the dawn chorus. Birds do it to express joy or proclaim territory or attract mates. In May the landscape exudes abundant life. There's nothing else like it.

Most of our birds are tropical birds that come here for the summer to nest and to feast on Canada's good bugs. This is a yellow warbler, feeding its young.

should have seen the faces of my friends who hadn't done much prairie canoeing before.

We had a good long look at this old, old snake. You could see it had been scarred, maybe chewed by a coyote or clawed by a great horned owl.

There are countless creatures that make a living in or near the riparian forests beside Alberta's rivers. There are raccoons that use the river edges as highways. Near the Milk River, hoary marmots, eagles, and owls sit or nest and watch you paddle by from the eroded features of the sandstone cliffs. We've also watched Canada geese, spotted sandpipers, mergansers, goldeneyes, willets, and godwits on Alberta's rivers.

When Dee and I do solo canoe trips together on the prairies, we paddle along keeping our conversation down to whispers. You see more wildlife if you are quiet. We'll glide around the corner and a mule deer or beaver may be looking at us. We've even seen pronghorn antelope swimming across the river in front of us.

Some of the wildlife that we see along the rivers has been dead for thousands or millions of years. We have found ammonites around rock bluffs that would be as big as birdbaths if they were all in one piece. These beautiful ammonites are relics of the ocean that used to wash over this part of the world. We have also found fossilized shark's teeth in the eroded hoodoos of the South Saskatchewan River. Of course we've found all kinds of dinosaur bones throughout Dinosaur Provincial Park and the Red Deer River Valley. We once hiked up through a coulee to find a long bone of a hadrosaur that was probably 65 million years old. It was about 1 meter (3 ft.) long!

Wildlife, living and fossilized, continues to keep bringing me back to prairie rivers with my canoe. Over the years, I have developed a passion for these southern Alberta river systems that only grows deeper each year I explore them.

This golden-mantled marmot looked out at us from the protection of the sandstone cliffs above the Milk River in Southern Alberta.

The racoon gets its English name from the Algonquian word *arakun*, meaning "he scratches with his hand."

BRIAN'S NOTES

A coulee is a ravine with sloping sides. The word "coulee" is from the French and means "to flow." In the spring, many coulees do indeed have creeks flowing through them because of melting snow or because the water table is high and water is pulsing out of the ground. The flowing water is what formed the coulees in the first place.

LET SLEEPING HIPPOS LIE

Dee and I once had a scary experience on a river with an enormous mammal: a hippopotamus. We were about to enter Mupata Gorge in Zimbabwe. This is where the whole Zambezi River narrows to about 100 meters (328 ft.) wide. The current was starting to pick up. We had just finished paddling through an area we call Hippo Alley, which has hundreds of hippos. You have to be very careful when you canoe through hippo territory. They are big animals, and they own the river.

I was sitting in the canoe thinking about what a perfect day it had been, when suddenly a hippo bit through our canoe.

His whole head came up and crushed the side of the boat! He knocked out a piece of fiberglass as wide as his face. His lips pushed my leg over, and his tusks came through the bottom of the boat only centimeters from my feet. I could see the follicles of hair on his nose, the pores on his skin, the water streaming off his face. All the details are forever burned in my brain.

As you can imagine, I was absolutely shocked and paralyzed with fear and surprise. This hippo looked up

Mother hippos help their babies rise to the surface to breathe as they teach them how to swim. Young hippos can only stay under the water for about 30 seconds, but adults can stay submerged up to 6 minutes.

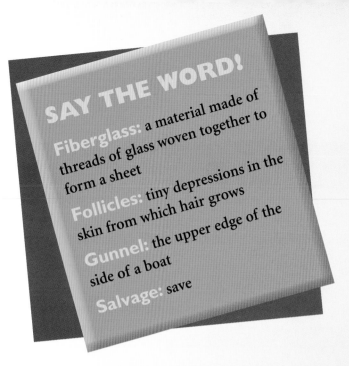
at me, and I could see his eyes open a little wider. I think I surprised the hippo as much as he surprised me. He took one chomp out of the side of the canoe, opened up his mouth, hit the boat again and chomped down and knocked out a bit more fiberglass. Then the hippo opened up his mouth and gave one backwards flick with his head, and our whole boat flipped upside down.

Thankfully the hippo didn't attack again. He just disappeared.

The hippo's reaction was an automatic response. I'm sure he had been dead asleep, and we had woken him up as we passed. Dee and I had been paddling along quietly, careful not to bang our paddles against the boat, not wanting to disturb the wildlife. We didn't warn the hippo we were coming. Had we made a little bit of noise, this probably never would have happened.

The sound of a paddle hitting a canoe gunnel is a very familiar sound to these hippos. If we had just tapped the side of the canoe once, the hippo would have known we were there. He would have gotten out of the way, or he

would have surfaced and looked at us, and we would have moved out of the way. But we woke up this sleeping hippo as he came to the surface for a breath. He did what was natural for him to do.

So, there we were, upside down, and the river current was picking up. I swam right up to the front of the canoe, and Dee was trying to figure out what had happened. I said, "We were hit by a hippo," just as I saw my paddle go by. Dee was going to go after the paddle but I insisted we stay with the canoe. We held onto the canoe and started working our way toward shore.

Finally that lovely feeling of gravel hit my fingers as I touched the bottom of the river. We both stood up right away and pulled the canoe in to get out of the danger zone, where crocodiles might take us. We dragged the

Male hippos will display their big teeth in a threatening way to warn other males to stay away from their territory. Sometimes just the threat of those teeth will scare other males away. Hippos are armed and potentially dangerous!

canoe onto shore, flipped it over, and then we gave each other a long hug.

Now we had to figure out what to do next. We were soaking wet, as was everything we had tied to the canoe, including our food. We picked up the pieces of the broken canoe and carried everything up on the shore to let the sun dry it out.

Hippos spend most of their day basking on sandbars, or in the water. They eat at night, when they may travel up to 32 kilometers (20 mi.) along the water's edge. Grass kept short by hippo grazing is known as a "hippo lawn."

Hippos can walk on river and lake bottoms, creating pathways that help to keep waterways moving. They have webbed feet that are great for both river-bottom walks and for supporting their big bodies on land.

Fortunately I had a fiberglass repair kit with a newspaper sheet worth of fiberglass. As Dee sorted out the gear and determined what food we could salvage, I set my attention to fixing the canoe. It was split right up to the middle of the boat.

I took the sheet of fiberglass in the shape of a big smiling hippo mouth and forced that back into place. We hadn't lost our garbage, which we had secured into the canoe, so I opened up tin cans to patch the holes where the tusks went through the bottom.

Within an hour the canoe was fixed. We turned it over and loaded it back up. By then the fiberglass had set well enough to get back into the river. Then Dee and I looked at each

other and decided not to let one bad encounter with a hippo destroy our relationship with the Zambezi. And we never did.

We are more careful now when we are paddling through Hippo Alley, no question.

It's often the individual hippo that you need to watch for. If you encounter a male with lots of females around him, he'll be the nicest hippo you'll ever want to meet. But a lone male who is trying to acquire territory to attract females is a

In the early 1980s, Mupata Gorge (shown here) was slated to be the site for a new dam, which would have flooded an important nature area, Mana Pools. A group called The Zambezi Society helped get Mupata Gorge off the dam site list, and saved Mana Pools, now a World Heritage Site.

hippo that you have to be cautious of. For example, we know 2 hippos on the Zambezi, Harvey the Happy Hippo and Henry the Mad Hippo. As you might be able to guess, we always avoid Henry's territory!

I suppose when you have an experience like this one, it forces you to respect wild creatures a little bit more. It's their home that we're invading when we hike, camp, or canoe. We are merely guests in the wilderness, so we can't hold a grudge against any creature that we might surprise or annoy. Dee and I still have a happy relationship with hippos, and we still paddle the Zambezi River almost every year.

BRIAN'S NOTES

When a hippo's top tusks and lower tusks come together, they slice like garden shears, so they can graze on riverside plants with ease. The tusks are razor sharp, like two machetes coming together.

Hippos can sleep underwater. They automatically rise to the surface to breathe, even if they are sleeping.

STAMPEDES AND MUD BATHS AT SECRET SPRINGS

Secret Springs is a very special place in Mana Pools National Park, Zimbabwe. I doubt it is even marked on a map. The spring is a little trickle of water that bubbles a meter wide and maybe 7 centimeters (3 in.) deep out of 2 or 3 different locations on a strip of sandstone-walled valley. In the rainy season, the springs bubble up into a gushing creek that flows into the Zambezi River, about 60 kilometers (37 mi.) away. "Secret Springs" isn't its real name, but I keep that to myself. Guides and other Zimbabweans go there to find a bit of peace away from touristy areas. They keep it to themselves, too.

This little ribbon of water that bubbles cool and crystal clear is the life-giving water for

If the elephant got this muddy, imagine what Garth and I looked like when we emerged from the water hole!

Garth Thompson and I, photographing elephants from inside a water hole. Don't try this at home!

in hot pursuit! They were so close I thought that the leopard was going to land in my lap. The leopard got away into the thick bush, and the lion stopped, turned around, and walked back down to the springs.

Not all animals at the springs are as lucky as that leopard was. We once happened across 6 lions on a buffalo in the middle of the spring. We sat above the sandstone cliff with a perfect view of the buffalo kill and watched. The lions ate all night. At sunrise, with their bellies so big they could barely get out of the valley, they left. All that remained was a carcass and a skull.

Then, we watched 3 different species of vultures arrive. For the next few hours they literally cleaned the bones. That night the

thousands of animals in the area. Wildlife just seems to drip out of the woods and come down to this little water source. And with all the animal traffic, you just never know what's going to happen.

When we camp at Secret Springs, we always settle in a spot with very few animal prints or spoor on the ground, so we can stay out of the way. Even so, one year, we were saying goodbye to our friend Garth at our campsite. We were setting up our table for a farewell toast, when we looked up, and there was a wall of elephants, both females and young! We were obviously in their way so we hurried down to a ravine to allow them to pass.

The elephants finally moved on, and we settled back down.

No sooner had we sat down to toast Garth, than a leopard came running out of the bush at full steam. The incredible throaty growl of the leopard told us it was terrified. Right behind it was a huge lion

BRIAN'S NOTES

When warthogs come down to the waterhole to drink, they don't seem a bit nervous. I think they take visual cues from the antelope in the area, watching them for any signs of danger. They're smart animals. If the antelope aren't barking or snorting, or running, then they feel safe enough to go for a drink. Still, whenever we've been at secret springs, lions have usually picked off at least one or two warthogs.

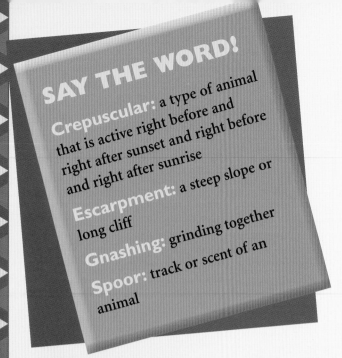
watching the bull elephants come down to the springs in the afternoon and dig their own wells. After digging they take in trunkful after trunkful of water, often drinking up to 150 liters (40 US gal.) of water in a day. Then they make mud wallows and cover themselves in mud.

In the morning, when the elephants are finished with the wells, Dee and I walk out and find the best one. Using my coffee mug, I slurp off the elephant snot that always floats on top, and then we fill up several big jugs of water from the well.

We use the first couple of jugs, filled with water as clean as we can hope for, for drinking and cooking. We stash the other jugs under

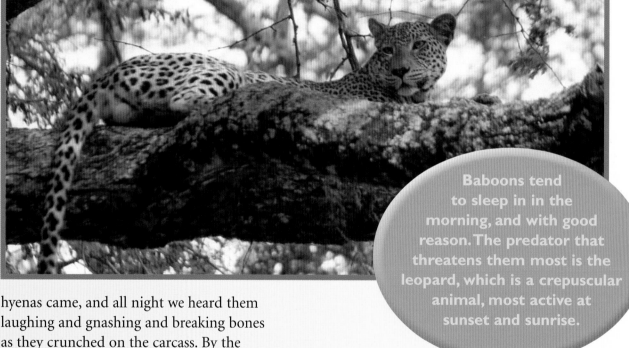

Baboons tend to sleep in in the morning, and with good reason. The predator that threatens them most is the leopard, which is a crepuscular animal, most active at sunset and sunrise.

hyenas came, and all night we heard them laughing and gnashing and breaking bones as they crunched on the carcass. By the following morning all that were left were 2 marabou storks picking up bits of flesh and bone and the skull of the buffalo. It was almost like the storks were a couple of janitors cleaning up after a really good party!

The joy of Secret Springs is that it feels like you're the only person in a world of wildlife. One special treat for us always is

trees to keep them shaded, then we use them later for showers or to wet down our clothing. With our water needs for the day taken care of, we can go ahead and find a spot in the shade, downwind so our scent won't carry, get comfortable in our chairs, and wait for the daily show of wildlife at the springs.

When elephants have left a well site, they also leave behind a lot of dung! The dung is a free meal for baboons, which come down from the trees and go from dollop to dollop, pulling it apart and eating the bits and pieces that weren't digested by the elephants.

An easy way to find your way around is to walk from big baobab tree to big baobab tree. It was on a walk like this that we found the baobab tree trap.

The Case of the Baobab Baboon Trap

One year, while walking around the baobab trees at Secret Springs, Dee and I came across a huge baobab that was hollow inside but open high up at the top. We discovered baboon skulls along with lots of long bones and ribs and vertebrae hidden within. We became naturalist detectives to try to understand what had happened.

At first we figured a leopard probably was eating the baboons in the treetop near the hole in the trunk. The carcasses likely slipped into the hole when the leopard was finished. But when leopards kill baboons, they grip the back of their skulls. On baboon skulls we'd found before, we always saw puncture holes where the leopard's teeth had gone through the skull. None of these skulls had any such holes in them. It may be that the killing technique of this leopard was different, but Dee and I started thinking about other possibilities.

Baboons love to eat baobab pods. Maybe every so often a baboon fell down this hole while eating these pods. Maybe it was curious about the hole or dropped a pod inside and then slipped in. The inside of the baobab was smooth, so perhaps once the baboon was inside, it was unable to get out.

We didn't truly solve the mystery, but it was an interesting puzzle to ponder as we hiked through the baobab trees.

PETER THE GREAT AND THE INK-BLACK RIVER

When the Calgary Zoo and the Georgetown Zoo in Guyana—the only English-speaking country in South America—teamed up, we were able to do great things. Together, we developed great education programs so the Georgetown Zoo could help the Guyanese people to understand the importance of the wildlife in their own backyard.

Eighty percent of Guyana is untouched tropical forest. There are not many countries in the world that can boast that. To highlight this, the Calgary Zoo took a couple of tour groups into Guyana to help with the country's new ecotourism program. It also gave Dee and me a chance to explore Guyana's outback.

One of the people we met in Guyana's tropical forest is a woman named Diane (pronounced Dee-ann) McTurk. She lives on and runs a cattle ranch called Karanambo Ranch on the Rupununi River. The ranch has a few wonderful, thatch-roofed guesthouses and an ecotour program.

Of all the world's known 5,743 amphibian species, about 1,856 are considered to be globally threatened. Because frogs use their skin to breathe and spend much time in the water, they are particularly susceptible to changes in both water and land environments.

Diane has come to the otters' rescue. Over the last 25 years, she has picked up orphaned baby river otters or otters in need of help and taken them into her care. She feeds them and cares for them and takes them to the river to swim every day. Eventually wild otters adopt

Giant anteaters have a keen sense of smell and a fine sense of hearing. These solitary animals need to be able to hear predators, such as pumas and jaguars, sneaking up on them.

The first time we went to Diane's ranch, we came in by boat through a windswept river. We saw black caiman, an endangered species of crocodile, slipping into the water off white sand banks. Huge Jabiru storks flew overhead. And somewhere in the Rupununi while we were crossing to the ranch, giant river otters were also swimming.

When we went to stay with Diane, Dee and I became instantly enchanted by her and her work. While a rancher, she is also the Jane Goodall of the rare giant river otters, locally known as "water dogs." These amazing creatures only live in Guyana's most out-of-the way, and unpeopled places. They have been hunted to near extinction.

Giant river otters use their long, muscular tails and webbed feet to maneuver in the water. They prefer to stay in slow-moving parts of rivers, but will follow their food, crabs and fish, to other areas, too.

the orphaned babies. Diane has had a tremendous success rate of getting otters back into the wild. Through her work she has also showed the local people that otters are smart, playful, loving creatures.

Before, fishermen and the community saw the otters as nuisances and competition for fish. Diane gives personality to these animals that were once considered an enemy. This has helped protect the population of otters in the area. And she has instilled a sense of respect for otters in the local children, who help Diane care for the baby otters at the ranch.

When we stayed with her, Diane introduced us to an odd otter named Peter the Great. Diane kept Peter for a couple of years at her ranch, and they were great friends. Peter

Stung by a Stingray

On one of my last days with Diane McTurk, I was walking in the shallows and stepped on a stingray. It was no bigger than a teacup saucer. I could feel its tail come up and hit me—BANG, BANG, BANG—very quickly 3 times on the side of my foot, injecting poison every time. It knocked me right off my feet! I limped back to Diane's ranch, which was about a 10-minute walk away.

By the time I got to the ranch, the pain was excruciating. I lay down on the hammock and for the next hour was in more pain than I ever believed the body could handle. It was like having the jagged end of a broken glass bottle ground into my foot, over and over again.

I asked if there was any traditional medication that would help. Everyone avoided eye contact and only said, "All you can do is drink rum. Lots of rum." I found out later that if somebody from the village steps on a stingray, an infection usually settles in. Then gangrene often occurs followed by amputation or even death. They were looking at me like I was a dead man.

I eventually fell asleep. The next day the pain was gone, and a huge blister the size of a chicken's egg had grown. Fortunately I was on my way back to North America. There I saw specialists who were able to clean and treat the wound. For 3 months my foot was in a solid cast so the skin could grow properly. Each week I had the cast removed so the specialists could clean the wound. Then a new cast went on. It was an incredibly painful reminder of how careful you have to be in a new landscape. It's a lesson I'll never forget! Lesson learned? Always do the "stingray shuffle," which makes the rays flap harmlessly away.

The mouth of Guyana's Essequibo River, about 27 kilometers (17 mi.) wide, separates mangrove tree and coastal forests in the west from farmlands and populated areas in the east.

even had a special bed in the cabin right next to Diane's. Everyday Diane took Peter down to the river where he'd spend time with a couple of children whose job it was to supervise Peter. Diane also hired a fulltime fisherman to catch fish to keep Peter fed.

Dee and I had a blast swimming with Peter. He was all over us in the inky-black water. He would be under the water and you'd wonder where he was. Then he would pop up and swim over, kiss us full on the lips, then climb on our backs and try to push our heads under the water.

I later went back to Guyana with a Discovery Television crew, figuring there was a good chance that we'd capture these otters on film.

Every day we went out, and Diane would yell the names of the otters at the top of her voice. Finally we had success. Two otters that had just been adopted by wild otters appeared out of the bush for a visit. We got out of our canoes, and the otters were all around us. The Discovery Channel team got great footage of these amazing giant river otters. I was thrilled to share this special place and these special animals with the rest of the world.

BRIAN'S NOTES

The Rupununi River is often referred to as the black waters of south America. The water is dark because it is dyed black from the tannins in the river. Tannins are chemicals that come out of the roots of the trees on the riverbank. You really can't see through the water. This makes it a great place to play hide-and-seek with river otters.

Guyana's rainforests cover about 17 million hectares (42 million acres). Dee and I were able to explore some of this vast outback of forest—the trees were amazing.

MY DREAM JOB

When I was going to college, I applied to be a wildlife interpreter in Southern British Columbia at the Creston Wildlife Centre near Creston, BC. When I found out that I got the job, I was so excited. It was my dream job.

I made my way to Creston amazed at my good luck. I had been a nature nut since I was 12 years old; it was like the job was made for me! I began by designing talks and

Owls, like this great horned owl, eat, and then a few hours later they cough up a pellet that contains the skull and the bones of whatever it's been eating. Nothing satisfies me more than finding an owl pellet in the woods and opening it up to see what the owl had been eating.

programs for kids and families that pointed out what wildlife was in the area. I also talked about how natural elements like water and sun and land work together with the wildlife to create an ecosystem. When I worked at the centre, I lived in a trailer my parents loaned me, which I parked on 8 hectares (20 acres) of land just a kilometer away from the centre. I spent three amazing summers there.

The focus of the Creston Wildlife Centre was the Kootenay River and the marshland in Duck Lake.

We used big, wooden, freighter canoes that were about 6 meters (20 ft.) long to take groups on long trips. On these trips, we told the story of the river and the pond systems, which are on the migration path called the Pacific Flyway. I would point out and explain the wildlife on either side of the canoe and in the water.

I especially loved to show everyone a certain heron rookery along the river. Everyone was excited about seeing those herons. After all, heron rookeries have been slowly disappearing as

centre so we could care for them and hopefully release them back into the wild. One day someone brought in a western grebe. It had been flying at night after a rainstorm, and it saw the road beside Kootenay Lake glistening. In the moonlight, the road must have looked like it was full of water. The grebe came down and landed on the road and couldn't take off again. Like loons, grebes have to run along the water for a long time before they become airborne.

We fed the grebe and looked it over. We had to hold it far away from our eyeballs because grebes have beaks like sabers, designed to spear fish quickly. Still, we got a good look at its brilliant ruby-red eyes and sharp bill. Then we took this exquisite bird back to the lake and let it go.

Another time, the biologist at the centre came into my office with a cardboard box and said, "Here Brian, take care of this."

Heron are very sensitive to human development in their nesting grounds. They will abandon a nesting site if they are harassed too much.

people build more and more houses close to their habitat. We would paddle past the heron rookery in absolute silence and watch these beautiful birds. We could hear the youngsters cackling to the adults. With binoculars we could see the young grab the adults' bills and shake back and forth until the adult regurgitated its food. We'd talk about birds barfing up half-digested fish and we'd all get a gross laugh out of it! Then we would push off and let the current carry us away.

I also took groups to Duck Lake to see the western grebe. This bird is on the red list, which means it is very close to becoming an endangered species. In spring, we watched them doing their mating dance. They would race across the lake like high-speed motorboats with their whole bodies out of the water and their heads held back in an S-curve. It was great to watch the grebes in action. One time I even got to see a grebe up close.

People often brought injured wildlife to the

BRIAN'S NOTES

Western grebes need water beneath them to take off. This is because their legs are positioned far back to help them deep-dive for food. A mallard can burst straight up into the air. Grebes, cormorants, and loons all have to run along the water before they can gain air.

Because so many turtles have been killed crossing the roads near the ponds in Creston Valley, there are now signs up on the highway which read: Turtle Crossing.

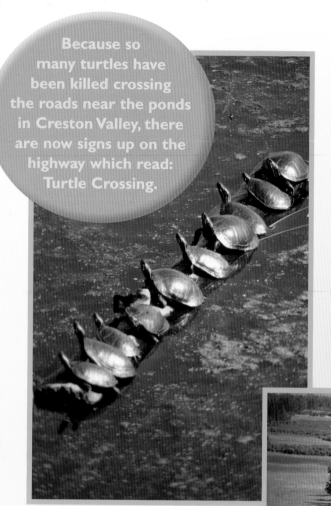

I canoed so much when I was an interpreter that I occasionally flushed secretive American bitterns out of the thick reeds. If a bittern is disturbed, it points its beak up to the sky and stands spread-eagle with its legs holding onto reeds, absolutely still.

One time I was driving to work, and a bittern was crossing the road. I stopped the car and the bittern did what nature told it to do: freeze and put its beak up to the sky. I sat in my car and watched for a good 35 seconds before I could

The Creston Valley Wildlife Centre sits amidst some marshlands that are a link in a chain of wetlands stretching from the Arctic Ocean to California. This chain is important to migrating birds.

It was a great horned owl that had accidentally landed on Duck Lake. I went to the butcher's and got some big chunks of meat for it. I could tell by the way it swallowed the morsels whole that there was nothing wrong with this owl.

That night I gave a presentation on owls at the campsite near the centre, and at the end of the evening I told everybody I had a special treat. We turned off the lights so the owl wouldn't get disoriented. Then I opened up the box, reached in with my gloved hand, and brought the owl out. The owl looked at all the people and, with one swish of its huge wings, it flew over the campers' heads and disappeared into the forest.

SAY THE WORD!

Endangered: in danger of extinction, especially when formally called "endangered" by a government or conservation group

Regurgitated: threw up

Rookery: a breeding ground for certain birds

Turtle Eggs in the Driveway

I was coming home from work at the centre one night in the middle of summer and I found a western painted turtle in my driveway. She had urinated on the road to soften up the soil, and she was digging a hole. I knew what this meant! I hurried up to my trailer and grabbed my flash camera, came back to the turtle, and until 3 AM I sat with the turtle and took pictures as she dug the hole and then laid eggs into it.

The eggs were beautiful, porcelain-like globes. After one or two eggs fell into the hole, the turtle would arch up and gently tamp the eggs into place, then she would lay more eggs. Of course these eggs are not hard like bird's eggs—they are tough and leathery. When she was finished laying them, the turtle karate-chopped the ground back and forth with her legs until you couldn't tell where the hole was. Then she left. I marked the place with a stick, then built a little cage around it so the raccoons wouldn't dig up the eggs. Later that fall I was able to watch and photograph the youngsters coming up and out of their nest.

> When it was time for the turtle eggs in my driveway to hatch, I dug up the soil above them, thinking the soil would be too hard for them to dig through. Success! The turtles came out of their shells and made their way to the ponds.

see it realizing that it was out in the open. It slowly pulled its head back into its body and slunk off the road. It was so funny! It almost looked embarrassed as it disappeared into the brush.

Southern British Columbia held so many great bird adventures for me. Those 3 years of working in and around the waterways of the Creston Valley taught me how to really respect and observe wildlife. It was the perfect job for a budding naturalist like me, and I learned a lot from it.

> A bittern chick in the Creston Valley. Bitterns still migrate to Creston Valley's ponds to raise their young.

A SACRED HIPPO ISLAND

In *Amazing Animal Adventures Around the World*, I talk about my 2001 visit to the Wechiau Community Hippo Sanctuary located along the Black Volta River in Ghana, West Africa. Wechiau protects one of two hippo populations in Ghana. It is a place where people are doing a wonderful job of living with the wildlife in their backyard, which just happens to be a river.

Wechiau is an amazing place—when you are there, you are experiencing wildlife and culture at the same time. When you wake up, you see people going out to their fields, kids on foot, men on bicycles. You hear the pounding of the "fu-fu," the rhythmic toonk-toonk, toonk-toonk of the pounding of yam.

To experience the wildlife, you hire a guide and walk about 2 kilometers (1 mi.) down to the river and get into a boat. The tree platform that Dee and I slept in during our first visit is still there, and so are two others. If you sleep out there you can hear hippos sloshing around during the night, bats feeding above you, and the magic of Ghana all around.

Rivers are often amazing pockets of life because they create a variety of places for animals and plants to live. There are backwaters, slow-moving pools, oxbows, and ponds from overflowing rivers, the river edge, the deep river itself, the forest along the edge, and the forest and grassland just beyond that.

There are over 200 bird species at Wechiau. You can see both aquatic and savannah birds here—pygmy kingfishers (like this one) and violet turacos in the water, and hornbills, hoopoes, and barbets in the savannah.

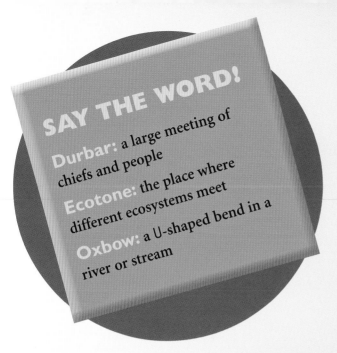

SAY THE WORD!

Durbar: a large meeting of chiefs and people

Ecotone: the place where different ecosystems meet

Oxbow: a U-shaped bend in a river or stream

Where a series of ecosystems meet is called an ecotone—and in and around ecotones, diversity goes through the roof! However, because of people, much of the wildlife along the Black Volta is now gone. But a special island called Tankara Island, in the middle of the Black Volta near Wechiau, and the area around it, has been a pocket of wildlife for centuries. It's an amazing story.

Four hundred years ago there were people hunting people in Ghana. Slave traders from all over Europe took turns living in castles on the coast of West Africa.

The slave traders paid local people living on the coast to go inland to capture people and bring them back as slaves. These people were shipped all over the world—to South America, the Caribbean, the United States, and other places. It was a horrible time.

At Wechiau, whenever the local people got wind that there were slave raiders coming in, they would race to Tankara Island and hide there. The people still believe there is a spirit living on the island that covers your trail when you set foot on it. No one who hid on Tankara Island was ever found by raiders. Hiding there worked, for hundreds of years. So, the local land priest declared that the island was sacred. No hunting or cutting of the trees or plants was allowed on the island.

This law, or taboo, continues today. The Wechiau Hippo Sanctuary, in fact, was started by the chiefs in the area to make sure that the island and the area around it would continue to be held sacred. The chiefs worked with their people to make the park a reality, and as they did, they started to learn about conservation.

The chiefs also talked to a man named John Mason, who heads an organization in Ghana called the Nature Conservation and Research Centre (NCRC). He helped the chiefs put together a conservation plan for the

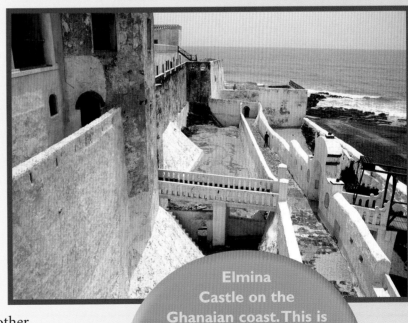

Elmina Castle on the Ghanaian coast. This is one of the slave castles built by Europeans trading in slaves. It is a relic of a horrific time in Ghanaian history.

sanctuary. And, then the Calgary Zoo got involved with John Mason and sent a conservation hero named Donna Sheppard to Ghana. Donna helped the sanctuary get on its feet. As a result, Tankara Island is still chock-full of life. In fact, when tourists go to Wechiau, they often find a large herd of wallowing hippos near the island or along the riverbank.

In six years, the hippo sanctuary has come a long way—tourists and scientists come from all over the world to see and study the hippos, birds, and other wildlife. By helping the animals, the people of Wechiau have also helped themselves.

Since becoming involved with the Wechiau Hippo Sanctuary, the Calgary Zoo has helped to fund a few important projects there. In 2005, a school for the Wechiau community children was started, thanks to the fundraising efforts of a woman named Heather Graham. The school is special because it is made of

There are only about 7,000 hippos in 19 countries in West Africa. East Africa has about 70,000 hippos, and southern Africa has about 80,000.

bricks that the community children had made themselves.

A lighting project is underway at Wechiau, too. My brother, John Keating, is working with the chiefs to ensure that eventually all 550 homes within the sanctuary will be lit by LED lights, powered by the sun. And, with the help of many Albertans raising money, like 11-year-old Matthew Harding, water wells are also springing up in Wechiau. As the Wechiau-Naa, the paramount chief, said, "The hippos have given us education, light, and water—we must continue to give to the hippos."

The Wechiau Hippo Sanctuary has become an amazing example of modern-day conservation, involving people and the wildlife in their back-yard. Wechiau is so successful that the Calgary Zoo is investigating a few other pockets of wilderness in Ghana where similar community parks might work. It's been exciting to watch Wechiau evolve. It's even more exciting to think that Wechiau could be just the starting point of more amazing conservation work!

BRIAN'S NOTES

The town of Wechiau got its name from the Wechegii word "chiau," meaning "to cut." When the people settled in Wechiau, the area was covered in trees and there were many wild animals. The people had to cut down a clearing to create a safe place to live.

The Enskinment

My visit to Wechiau in 2004 was one of the most amazing adventures I've ever had. In September, Alex Graham, the Calgary Zoo director, and I were made honorary chiefs at Wechiau.

When we arrived in Ghana it was just like we were returning home. We were taken to Wechiau, where we were treated to a grand

Alex (right) and me after being enskinned as honorary chiefs at Wechiau.

durbar. At least 800 people were there to see our enskinment. The ceremony is called an enskinment because to be made chief, you sit on a stool placed on an antelope skin.

My heart was pounding with excitement. And I was so hot, you can't believe it. We were in equatorial Africa at its hottest and most humid. Yet, to be enskinned, I was dressed in 2 beautiful (but hot!) robes. Each of the robes weighed several kilograms. After

I was dressed, I was given a pair of HUGE pants that I put on and tightened around my waist. The waistline is so huge that you and three of your friends could fit in them!

With hand-tooled riding boots, a hat, and a carved walking stick to complete my chief's regalia, the party began, with drumming and dancing like I've never seen.

The official ceremony ended at sunset (about 6 PM), after gifts were given. I was given about 300 kilograms (662 lb.) of yams. Seems strange, but yams are something that everybody can give. After a wonderful dinner under the only light bulb in the whole village, we went back to the sanctuary and slept in our mud huts.

We were exhausted but incredibly proud and happy. We were absolutely blown away at the honor we were given.

Alex and I understand the importance of being made chiefs. The only way we can retire from our special honor is by dying. As chiefs, Alex and I have agreed to continually serve our people. That's what you do when you are a chief. And that is what we intend to do.

CONSERVATION—IT'S UP TO YOU

If you'd like to learn more about or become involved in wildlife conservation, contact any or all of the following organizations.

Africa Rainforest and River Conservation
info@africa-rainforest.org 1-307-743-0077

Calgary Zoo
1300 Zoo Road, SE
Calgary, Alberta, Canada T2E 7V6
1-403-232-9333 www.calgaryzoo.ab.ca

Canadian Heritage Rivers System
c/o Parks Canada
Ottawa, Ontario, Canada K1A 0M5
1-819-994-2913 www.chrs.ca

Canadian Hydro Developers, Inc.
1324 - 17th Avenue SW, Suite 500
Calgary, Alberta, Canada T2T 5S8
1-403-269-9379 www.canhydro.com

Canadian Nature Federation
1 Nicholas Street, Suite 606
Ottawa, Ontario, Canada K1N 7B7
cnf@cnf.ca 1-613-562-3447
www.cnf.ca

**Canadian Parks and Wilderness
Society National Office**
880 Wellington Street, Suite 506
Ottawa, Ontario, Canada K1R 6K7
info@cpaws.org 1-800-333-WILD
www.cpaws.org

Canadian Wildlife Federation
350 Michael Cowpland Drive
Kanata, Ontario, Canada K2M 2W1
info@cwf-fcf.org 1-800-563-WILD
www.cwf-fcf.org

Creston Valley Wildlife Management Area
PO Box 640
Creston, British Columbia, Canada V0B 1G0
askus@crestonwildlife.ca 1-250-402-6900
www.crestonwildlife.ca

David Suzuki Foundation
2211 West 4th Avenue, Suite 219
Vancouver, British Columbia, Canada V6K 4S2
solutions@davidsuzuki.org 1-800-453-1533
www.davidsuzuki.org

Ducks Unlimited (Wetland Conservation)
Box 1160
Oak Hammock Marsh, Manitoba, Canada R0C 2Z0
1-800-665-3835 www.ducks.ca

Earthwatch International
3 Clock Tower Place, Suite 100
Box 75
Maynard, Massachusetts, USA 01754
1-800-776-0188 www.earthwatch.org

The Jane Goodall Institute (Canada)
Mr. Nicolas Billon, Executive Assistant
P. O. Box 477, Victoria Station
Westmount, Quebec, Canada H3Z 2Y6
nicolas@janegoodall.ca 1- 514-369-3384 (fax)
www.janegoodall.ca

Otter Conservation Center Inc.
250 Otter Conservation Road
Statesboro, Georgia, USA 30458
(912) 839-2100 or (912) 839-2550

The Zambezi Society
PO Box HG774, Highlands,
Harare, Zimbabwe
zambezi@mweb.co.zw
www.zamsoc.org

Cool Sites on the Web:
Species At Risk: www.speciesatrisk.ca
Space for Species: www.spaceforspecies.ca
National Park Service: Partnership Wild & Scenic Rivers
U.S. Department of the Interior:
http://www.nps.gov/ncrc/programs/pwsr/index.html
http://www.wilderness-safaris.com

INDEX

Cover and interior design by John Luckhurst
Cover and interior illustrations by Brian and Dee Keating
Edited by Rennay Craats
Copyedited by Meaghan Craven
Proofread by Lesley Reynolds
Scans by ABL Imaging

The publisher gratefully acknowledges the support of The Canada Council for the Arts and the Department of Canadian Heritage.

THE CANADA COUNCIL | LE CONSEIL DES ARTS
FOR THE ARTS | DU CANADA
SINCE 1957 | DEPUIS 1957

We acknowledge the financial support of the Government of Canada through the Book Publishing Industry Development Program (BPIDP) for our publishing activities.

Printed in Hong Kong

10 09 08 07 06 / 5 4 3 2 1

First published in the United States in 2006 by
Fitzhenry & Whiteside
121 Harvard Avenue, Suite 2
Allston, MA 02134

Library and Archives Canada Cataloguing in Publication

Keating, Brian, 1955-
Amazing animal adventures in rivers / with Brian Keating.

(Going wild)
Includes index.
ISBN-13: 978-1-894856-88-1 (bound).
ISBN-10: 1-894856-88-0 (bound).
ISBN-13: 978-1-894856-89-8 (pbk.).
ISBN-10: 1-894856-89-9 (pbk.)

1. Stream animals—Juvenile literature. 2. Rivers—Juvenile literature.
I. Title. II. Series: Keating, Brian, 1955- Going wild.

QL145.K43 2006   j591.76'4
C2005-907168-0

Fifth House Ltd.
A Fitzhenry & Whiteside Company
1511, 1800-4 St. SW
Calgary, Alberta T2S 2S5

1-800-387-9776
www.fitzhenry.ca

ACKNOWLEDGEMENTS

There are many people who have inspired me in my work as a naturalist. A special mention first needs to be extended to the dozens of guides who have patiently taken me up and down rivers in so many parts of the world over the past 25 years. I would like to thank the dedicated guides at the Wechiau Hippo Sanctuary, and the chiefs, who made this riverine park a reality. My thanks to Donna Sheppard, my conservation partner in Ghana, who, along with the chiefs, is the powerhouse behind making the Wechiau Hippo Sanctuary a success. Thank you to Johnny Micas of Canadian Rivers Expeditions, who hired me to be the naturalist on a Tatshenshini River rafting expedition; to Diane McTurk in Guyana, who took me out onto the Rupununi River with my crazy filming friends to produce our TV show; and especially to my good friend Garth Thompson in Zimbabwe. He was the first professional naturalist to introduce me to the most magnificent river in the world: the mighty Zambezi.

Thanks go out to our Alberta canoeing buddies: Doug and Nancy, Jamie and Lisa, Eric and Sue, and Mark and Delia. They share Dee's and my desire to be out there, exploring and playing on and around our wilderness rivers. And most important, I would like to thank my wife Dee, who shares my love for these wild rivers and who is my dedicated travel and camping partner.

Thanks, of course, to the staff at Civilized Adventures, especially Denell, for making all this travel come true; to the Calgary Zoo, for hiring me in the first place to pursue these dreams; and to the wonderful ladies at Fifth House Publishers for making the book writing process so much fun! Charlene, Meaghan, and Simone: You Rock!

DON'T FORGET!
*Amazing Animal Adventures
    Around the World*
*Amazing Animal Adventures
    at the Poles*
*Amazing Animal Adventures
    in the Desert*